Instant Pot® Coo

50 Easy, Healthy, Low-Carb & Gluten-Free Instant Pot® Recipes for Beginners and Busy People!

low carb and gluten free

BONUS RECIPES INCLUDED!

Renil M. George

This cook book is dedicated to my baby girl, Sara Katherine. Daddy loves you; you are my inspiration to keep going every day!

I would also like to dedicate this to my fellow IPers who spent countless hours reviewing, offering feedback and helping to create some amazing recipes. This could not have been possible without you.

Thank you, I love you guys!

Once an IPer, always an IPer!

Book Description

If you are looking for a way to provide your family and loved ones with healthy meals that are not going to take too much of your precious time to prepare—this book is the answer to your prayers! Within these pages, you will find a wonderful collection of healthy recipes that will have your loved ones begging for more. Your Instant Pot® will be a great kitchen tool which will make your life a lot easier when it comes to preparing family meals that are full of beneficial ingredients to help you keep off the excess pounds and keep you and your loved ones healthy and strong.

We live in a fast-paced world. Often, just preparing a meal for our loved ones can feel challenging, especially after a long, hard day at work. Think of how nice it would feel to walk in the front door and smell the lovely aroma of dinner ready and waiting for you to dish out and enjoy with your loved ones. With a little planning and effort, this could be part of your daily lifestyle! Feel good, knowing you are offering your loved ones a great, healthy meal at the end of a tiring day. Not only will you be eating healthier, home-cooked meals with the Instant Pot® and the recipes in this cookbook, but you will save money when you avoid eating out at fast food restaurants. You'll also have more quality time to sit down with your loved ones and share a meal when you're not spending so much time in the kitchen.

This Instant Pot® Cookbook Offers Something for Everyone:

- Nutritional Facts
- Cooking Time
- Low-Carb Recipes
- Vegetarian Recipes
- Family Friendly Recipes
- Gluten-free Recipes
- Low-Fat Recipes
- Breakfast Recipes
- Lunch Recipes
- Dinner Recipes
- Bonus Recipes!

Thank you, everyone. If you liked this labour of love, please leave a review on Amazon.

"Stay Calm and IP On!"

Renil M. George

Introduction

I would like to thank and congratulate you for getting Instant Pot® Cookbook: 50 Easy, Healthy, Low-Carb & Gluten-free Instant Pot® Recipes for Beginners and Busy People! If you are someone who wants to make healthier choices in life, then a great way to start is by choosing foods which are beneficial to your health and well-being and adding them to your daily diet. An excellent way to provide yourself and your loved ones with healthy meals is to use Instant Pot® recipes that are quick and easy to prepare. In this recipe collection, I have combined easily-to-follow recipes with quick and healthy meals that offer the nutrition you need to sustain good health.

I have mainly focused on low-carb and gluten-free recipes in this collection. This book provides a mixture of different ethnically-based recipes. I hope to write a series of cookbooks, starting with this one and then following with others that are more specialized, such as a book on Spanish recipes.

We are going to explore a wide variety of wonderful tasting, Instant Pot® recipes which have wholesome, healthy ingredients. You may be surprised at how many different kinds of dishes you can prepare using your Instant Pot®. We will cover recipes from breakfast to dinner, and most can be made within 45 minutes. When you are making more one-pot meals, you will love how simple and easy cleanup is! You are going to love cooking with your Instant Pot® so much, you'll wonder how you ever got along in the kitchen without it!

Thanks again for getting this book. I hope you enjoy it!

Renil M. George

Your Free Gift!!

As an offer of appreciation and gratitude to my fellow IPers, and my readers, here is another 35 ADDITIONAL breakfast, lunch, and dinner Instant Pot® Recipes.

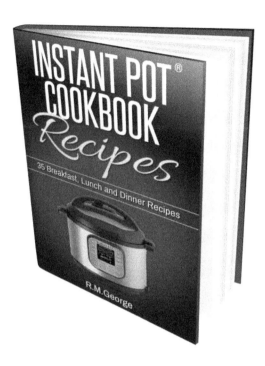

>>Click Here To Download *Instant Pot® Cookbook Recipes: 35 Breakfast, Lunch and Dinner Recipes*<<___

Table of Contents

Bonus Recipes!

Conclusion

Chapter 1 - Using Your Instant Pot® Pressure Cooker

The all-in-one features of the Instant Pot® make it a great cooking tool. Once you are more familiar with and comfortable using yours, you will find the meal possibilities endless. First, you should read through the manual that came with your Instant Pot® before you use your appliance. Keep your manual close at hand for future reference. You can also get a downloadable manual at InstantPot.com/benefits/specifications-and-manuals.

Why Should You Use a Pressure Cooker?

The answer to this is it all boils down to versatility and speed. With the build-up of steam, which then causes the pressure to rise within the pot along with the temperature, the effects of long braises, boils and simmers can be simulated by a pressure cooker within a short period of time. In the process, you will be able to save cooking time and energy without sacrificing the taste and texture of your food. This wonderful form of cooking was first invented in the 1600s in the form of a large cast iron vessel which had a lock top, and it continues to improve over time. After WWII there was a decline in the popularity of pressure cookers, but recently there has been a resurgence. New and improved models (introduced in the 90s) have shown that pressure cooking is a safe, fast and easy way to prepare nutritious, great tasting meals for you and your loved ones.

Benefits of Pressure Cooking

You are going to discover many benefits associated with pressure cooking your foods. The list compiled below is basically just the beginning. When you begin to expand on your pressure cooking knowledge and experience, your list will become longer.

Cook Food Fast

You can cut traditional cooking times by 70% when using your pressure cooker, making it a great appliance for preparing super-quick, healthy meals.

Preserving the Nutrition in Healthy Meals

Because less liquid is required to pressure cook your foods, they will be more nutritious than if you were to boil them, as fewer minerals will leak out of your foods into the liquid. With the shorter cook time, this also helps in preserving the vitamins inside your foods. Pressure cooking is an exceptionally healthy way to prepare your meals.

Little Fuss in Preparing Wonderful Meals

The pressure is automatically regulated in pressure cookers, and you can use a timer to monitor your cooking time. With these automated functions they are much easier to use than their stovetop counterparts. Also, their hands-off functionality makes them very user-friendly and safe. This is an appliance that you will love to have close at hand on your countertop.

One-Pot Meals

You can use a pressure cooker to turn out some great-tasting, healthy, one-pot meals. Not only will this significantly reduce your cooking time, but you will not lose the nutritional value of your foods. All you need to do is to throw your ingredients into the pot, turn it on, and let it work its magic! You can make healthy chili, hearty stews, or even a quick pasta dish in no time at all. At the end of the meal, you will have only one pot to wash.

Go Green

Pressure cookers are eco-friendly since they have a faster cook time and efficiently use energy. When you compare a pressure cooker to other methods of cooking, such as using the stovetop, they use two to three times less energy.

Electric Pressure Cooking

Many people find pressure cooking a bit intimidating based on the very thing which makes it an excellent way to prepare meals: all you need to do is put your food in the pot—do not try to peek—and allow it to do the work. We understand now how different foods will react under pressure and can offer accurate cook times, thus removing all the guesswork from preparing your meals with a pressure cooker. All you need to do is look at the recipe of your choice. Check to see if it involves browning or sautéing before you pressure cook it. Look to see what the pressure level should be and what the cook time should be. Below are listed the typical steps followed in a pressure cooker recipe.

1. In order to enhance the flavor of your foods, you will often use the Sauté function for sautéing or browning your meat before you pressure cook it. When you are using this function you will leave the top off.

2. Add in your recipe ingredients and then secure the lid by turning the steam release handle to the sealing position.

3. Now select the pressure level (either high or low) and the cook time according to the recipe manual. Your cooker will then automatically start.

4. When your pressure cooking is complete, turn off your cooker by selecting the Cancel function. Doing this will disengage the Warming function.

5. Use a quick release or a natural release. For a quick release, you release the steam manually. Make sure when doing this that you use extreme caution! Use a thick kitchen towel or oven mitt to turn the handle and quickly get out of the way while the steam releases. Using the quick release is good when you are cooking delicate items such as seafood. A natural release is performed when you select Cancel. You will then leave the Instant Pot® to sit until the float valve sinks, slowly releasing pressure and locking in the flavor. This process can take up to 10 minutes or more. A natural release is good to use with tough meats, stews, and sauces. Carefully remove the lid at the end of the steam release process.

If you are preparing foods that tend to foam, do not fill the pot too high. You should only fill the pot three-quarters full with any dish you prepare. Once you have completed cooking your meal remember the cooker is going to be hot. Use extreme caution when releasing pressure; steam can cause nasty burns if you are not careful. Use a thick oven mitt or towel to turn the handle then quickly get out of the way. Make sure to unplug your Instant Pot® when it is not in use.

Convert Your Favorite Dishes

You can prepare a wide range of dishes in your pressure cooker. Once you have tried the recipes in this collection, you may get itchy feet and want to convert some of your favorite stovetop recipes. You can convert most recipes if you keep a few things in mind, such as the following:

- **Reduce the Amount of Liquid**—Since pressure cookers do not allow evaporation like stovetop cooking, you will not need as much liquid. Adjust your recipe accordingly, but do not go under the minimum of one cup of liquid.
- **Decrease Your Cook Time**—A dish cooked in a pressure cooker will typically take one-third to one-half of the cooking time of a traditional stovetop recipe. Check the cook time chart and compare your recipe ingredients with it to find your cooking time.
- **Add Dairy Ingredients at the End**—If the recipe needs dairy, the general rule is to add it at the end, after pressure cooking is over. Dairy tends to scorch and foam when heated in a pressure cooker.
- **Thicken Recipe at End**—When using flour or cornstarch as thickeners, incorporate them after the pressure cooking is completed by using the Sauté function.
- **Do Not Overfill the Pot—P**ay attention to how big the recipe is and adjust it so as to not overfill the pot. Also remember that bigger recipes do not mean longer cook times. The pressure cooker will cook everything at the same rate. Consider experimenting with this pressure-cooking converter: HipPressureCooking.com/pressure-cooker-recipe-converter.
- **Consult Your Manual**—When using a pressure cooker it is a good idea to consult the manual often.

Your Instant Pot® is composed of an exterior pot that has a heating element inside of it and a control panel on the outside of it. The inner pot is where your food is placed during the cooking process. This fits nice and snug inside the exterior pot. The lid has a steam release and large handle. The valve for steam release is used when a quick release of steam is needed. This valve should be in the sealing position before you begin pressure cooking. Under the lid are a sealing ring, exhaust valve and float valve used to create a nice tight seal and regulate pressure within the Instant Pot®.

There are a number of cooking functions available with the Instant Pot®. You can adjust the cook time or the heat level by using the Adjust More (+) or Less (-) buttons on your Instant Pot®. The pressure key on this appliance will waver between high and low pressure for all the pressure cooking functions except when cooking rice. The most common setting is high pressure for most recipes; the low setting is used when you are cooking delicate foods such as seafood. Once the last key is pressed your Instant Pot® will begin to preheat in 10 seconds.

Manual

When you want to input your own settings from scratch, it is best to start with the manual setting. The recipes within this cookbook mainly call for using the manual function. You can then adjust the settings of time and pressure as needed.

Steam

This setting is designed to be used along with the metal steam rack. The steam function heats at full power, boils the water below and steams the food in the basket.

Meat/Stew

This is the best setting to use when making hearty meals with meats, cooking at a high pressure, and adjusting the time depending on the kind of meat you are using in the recipe. Check out the Cooking Time Charts when trying to determine cook times.

Bean/Chili

This function is specifically used for cooking dried beans at high pressure. You can adjust the time to suit how much you like your beans cooked.

Slow Cook

This is a wonderful option for those who have had a long, busy day and want dinner cooked and ready and waiting when they get home from work. When using this function, make sure to set the steam release to the venting position.

Sauté

The sauté function is great for making one-pot recipes. Use this function to soften veggies or brown meat before pressure cooking. It is also good for thickening sauces after pressure cooking is complete, as well. For slow simmering, it is best to set it on low. For sautéing and browning, it is best to set it on high.

Multigrain

It is easy to cook grains, such as wild or brown rice, at high pressure with the Instant Pot®. When cooking grains make sure to refer to the Cooking Time Charts to get the right amount of liquid needed to complete the recipe successfully, as well as the right amount of cook time. These are key elements to a successful end result.

Porridge

When using the porridge function, the normal setting is for rice porridge while the high setting is a mixture of grains and beans. Use natural release when using this function.

Poultry

This function is used when cooking chicken, duck, and turkey at high pressure. Consult your Instant Pot® manual or the Electric Pressure Cooking Time Charts when determining cook time for the recipe.

Rice

With this function, regular rice is cooked at low pressure. Cooking duration is automatically adjusted based on the amount of liquid and rice in the cooker, which allows for as little as one cup of rice to be prepared.

Yogurt

Homemade yogurt can be made using the Instant Pot® two-step function. Details can be found in the manual.

Soup

Using an electric pressure cooker is a great way to prepare soups and broths. Using the Soup function will prevent it from boiling too heavily.

There is a Delayed Cooking function and a Keep Warm feature on the Instant Pot®, allowing for perfectly timed meals. The pot's warming feature is automatically activated when the cooking timer runs out. To turn it off, select Cancel. To allow the pressure to release faster, turn off the warming feature after cooking is completed. Press Cancel when you have finished cooking any recipe in this book.

Cleaning & Caring for Your Instant Pot®

To keep your Instant Pot® in great working order for many years to come, give it a bit of TLC. Unplug it after each and every use. To clean the inner pot, use warm, soapy water or place it in the dishwasher. Clean the lid with a wet cloth and wipe dry. Remove the sealing ring and clean with soapy water if needed, then dry it before replacing it. You can also remove the steam release valve for cleaning. Use a dry cloth to wipe out the inside of the pot. When preparing strong smelling dishes, such as curries, your sealing ring will take on the strong smells. Be sure to clean it with warm, soapy water. You may choose to keep an extra sealing ring just for cooking aromatic dishes.

Safety Tips & Suggestions for Instant Pot®

It is always a good idea when cooking with your Instant Pot®, to keep a few safety tips in mind. Before using, check the bottom of the inner pot and the heating plate it sits upon. Make sure they are both clean and dry. Also, check to make sure the float valve, exhaust valve, and anti-block shield are also clean and free of any food. Check that the sealing ring is secure. Make sure the steam release handle is in the Sealing position. Do not overfill the pot when adding food. If you notice the Instant Pot® making unusual noises or emitting a burning smell, or if the power cord has become damaged, stop using it.

Chapter 2 - Instant Pot® Breakfast Recipes

1. Sausage & Cheese Frittata (Gluten-free)

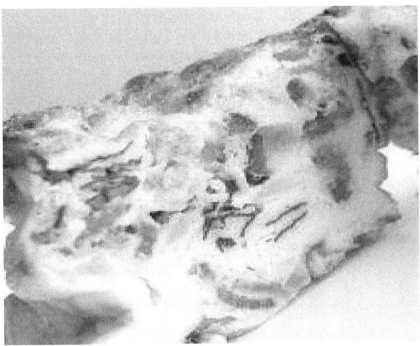

Prep Time: 15 minutes
Pressure: 17 minutes
Total: 40 minutes
Pressure Level: Low
Release: Quick
Per Serving: Calories: 282, Protein: 16g, Trans Fat: 0g, Saturated Fat: 12g, Total Carbs: 1g, Fiber: 0g, Sodium: 385g
Servings: 2-4

Ingredients:

- 1 ½ cups of water
- 1 tablespoon butter
- 4 eggs, beaten
- 2 tablespoons sour cream, light
- ½ cup sausage, cooked and crumbled
- ¼ cup old cheddar cheese, grated
- 2 scallions, chopped
- Salt and pepper to taste

Directions:

- Add water to empty Instant Pot® and place steam rack on top.
- Butter a 6-inch soufflé baking dish with handles.
- In a bowl, beat together eggs and sour cream.
- Add sausage, cheese, scallions, salt and pepper; mix well.
- Pour into buttered pan. Cover pan with foil and place on steam rack. Secure lid, select 'manual' and set on low pressure; cook for 17 minutes.
- Upon completion of cooking, use quick release.
- Carefully remove pan.
- If a browned top is desired, place under broiler for a few minutes.

2. Potato & Pepper Frittata (Gluten-free, Vegetarian, and Family Friendly)

Prep Time: 15 minutes
Pressure: 17 minutes
Total: 40 minutes
Pressure Level: Low
Release: Quick
Per Serving: Calories: 470, Protein: 19g, Saturated Fat: 10g, Trans Fat: 0g, Total Carbs: 38g, Fiber: 5g, Sodium: 315g
Servings: 2-4

Ingredients:

- 1 ½ tablespoons extra virgin olive oil
- 1 large yellow potato, cut into ¼-inch slices
- ½ yellow onion, cut into thin slices
- ½ red bell pepper, seeded and cut into ¼-inch rings
- 1 ½ cups water
- Butter for greasing
- 4 eggs, beaten
- 2 tablespoons sour cream, light
- Salt and pepper to taste

- ¼ cup Monterey Jack or old cheddar cheese grated

Directions:

- Select sauté and add oil to Instant Pot®.
- Once hot, add potato slices in one layer. Cook 4 minutes, then flip and cook other side for 2 minutes; remove.
- Add onion to the pot and cook for 2 minutes;
- Add bell pepper and cook for additional 2 minutes; remove from pot. Select Cancel.
- Add water to empty pot and place steam rack into pot.
- Butter a 6-inch soufflé dish.
- Beat eggs in a bowl and add sour cream; add salt and pepper to taste; mix well.
- Layer half of potatoes, bell pepper, and onion in prepared baking dish.
- Pour half of egg mixture over pepper and onion, then sprinkle with half of cheese. Repeat, ending with cheese on top.
- Cover with foil, place dish on steam rack. Secure lid, select 'manual' and set on low pressure; cook for 17 minutes.
- Use quick release once cooking is complete.

3. Eggs with Eggplant (Vegetarian, Family Friendly)

Prep Time: 30 minutes
Pressure: 10 minutes
Total: 50 minutes
Pressure Level: High
Release: Quick
Per Serving: Calories: 680, Protein: 31g, Saturated Fat: 5g, Trans Fat: 0g, Total Carbs: 87g, Fiber: 23g, Sodium: 1688mg
Servings: 2-4

Ingredients:

- 1 small eggplant, peeled, cut into ½-inch pieces
- 1 tablespoon salt
- 2 tablespoons extra-virgin olive oil
- 2 teaspoons garlic, minced
- 1 (28 oz) can crushed tomatoes (drain most of the liquid out)
- 1 teaspoon smoked paprika
- ¼ teaspoon red pepper flakes
- Fresh ground pepper to taste
- 4 eggs
- 1 tablespoon fresh parsley, chopped

- 4 slices rustic bread, for serving
- Hot sauce (optional), for serving

Directions:

- Put eggplant in bowl with salt and mix until coated.
- Spread onto a paper towel and let sit for 30 minutes.
- Press the moisture out using more paper towels, wiping salt away as you go.
- Preheat Instant Pot® by selecting Sauté. Add oil when hot. Add in eggplant, garlic, tomatoes, paprika, red pepper flakes and black pepper.
- Select 'manual' and set at high pressure; cook for 10 minutes.
- Use quick release once cooking is complete.
- Sauté the sauce. Crack eggs into a small bowl, gently slide onto top of sauce in pot.
- Cook, loosely covered, until eggs are set.
- Top with parsley; serve with bread and hot sauce.

4. Bacon & Egg Strata (Family Friendly)

Prep Time: 15 minutes
Pressure: 15 minutes
Total: 45 minutes
Pressure Level: High
Release: Natural
Per Serving: Calories: 321, Protein: 20g, Saturated Fat: 10g, Trans Fat: 0g, Total Carbs: 12g, Fiber: 1g, Sodium: 766mg
Servings: 4-5

Ingredients:

- 4 slices bacon
- 1 ½ cups water
- 1 tablespoon butter
- 3 large eggs, beaten
- 1 cup whole or 2% milk
- Salt and pepper to taste
- 3 cups stale, whole-wheat bread, cut into ¾-inch cubes
- ¼ cup sharp cheddar cheese, grated, plus 2 tablespoons for topping

Directions:

- Over medium heat in frying pan, crisp bacon on both sides.

- Place bacon on paper towel to drain.
- When cool, cut into small pieces.
- Add water to Instant Pot® and insert steam rack.
- Butter a 6-inch soufflé baking dish with handles; place into pot.
- In mixing bowl, whisk eggs, milk and seasoning; add in bread cubes and allow to sit for 5 minutes.
- Add ¼ cup of cheese and bacon to bread mixture; mix well and pour into prepared soufflé dish. Secure lid, select 'manual' and set at high pressure; cook for 15 minutes.
- Once cooking is finished, use natural release.
- Remove lid carefully to avoid condensation dripping onto meal.
- Remove soufflé dish with oven mitts.
- Optional: preheat oven broiler; top with remaining cheese and broil for 2 minutes.

Chapter 3 - Instant Pot® Lunch Recipes

5. Spanish Chicken Fajitas (Gluten-free)

Prep Time: 5 minutes
Pressure: 5 minutes
Total: 12 minutes
Pressure Level: High
Release: Quick
Per Serving: Calories: 330, Protein: 21g, Fat: 11g, Total Carbs: 23g, Fiber: 2g
Servings: 4

Ingredients:

- 1 tablespoon olive oil
- 2 white onions, chopped
- 2 teaspoons garlic, minced
- 1 pound chicken breasts, skinless and boneless
- 1 can tomatoes, diced
- 1 cinnamon stick
- 2 sweet red peppers, 1 cut into strips, 1 chopped
- 1 mild chili pepper, chopped
- ½ cup raisins
- 8 corn tortillas

-

Optional add-ins: shredded cheese, beans, red pepper flakes

Directions:

- Heat olive oil in Instant Pot®.
- Sauté onions, garlic, and chicken until browned.
- Add in tomatoes, cinnamon stick, peppers, and raisins.
- Secure lid; set at high pressure and cook for 5 minutes; use quick release to remove heat from pot.
- Serve mixture with corn tortillas and other optional add-ins.

6. Cheese-Stuffed Burgers (For Gluten-free, Omit Hamburger Bun)

Prep Time: 10 minutes
Pressure: 5 minutes
Total: 30 minutes
Pressure Level: High
Release: Quick
Per Serving: Calories: 519, Protein: 53g, Fat: 34g, Total Carbs: 2g, Fiber: 1g
Servings: 2

Ingredients:

- 1 pound lean ground beef
- 1 tablespoon Worcestershire sauce
- Salt and pepper to taste
- Garlic powder
- 2 slices smoked Gouda
- 1 cup water

Optional toppings: sautéed onions, tomato, lettuce, pickles, sprouts, avocados

Directions:

- Mix ground beef, Worcestershire sauce, salt, pepper and garlic powder.

- Form into 4 balls; flatten with plate; top 2 patties with 1 slice each of smoked Gouda and top with remaining 2 patties; seal edges.
- Pour water into Instant Pot® and insert steam rack; place burgers on top of steam rack.
- Secure lid; set at high pressure and cook for 5 minutes.
- Release heat using quick release.
- Take out steam tray; serve burgers with or without buns along with additional toppings as desired.

7. Chicken Noodle Soup (Family Friendly)

Prep Time: 10 minutes
Pressure: 21 minutes
Total: 32 minutes
Pressure Level: High
Release: Quick
Per Serving: Calories: 301, Protein: 21g, Fat: 13g, Total Carbs: 23g, Fiber: 0g
Servings: 8

Ingredients:

- 6 cups of water
- 3 chicken breasts
- 2 cups carrots, diced
- 2 cups celery, diced
- 2 cups winter squash, pureed
- 3 teaspoons chicken bouillon
- 1 teaspoon celery seed
- 2 cups yellow onion, chopped
- 1 tablespoon fresh parsley, chopped
- 1 teaspoon onion salt
- 2 cans (10.75 oz each) cream of chicken soup
- 8 ounces egg noodles

- Salt and pepper to taste

Directions:

- Add all ingredients to Instant Pot® except for cream of chicken soup and egg noodles.
- Secure lid, set at high pressure and cook for 21 minutes.
- Use quick release when cooking time is completed.
- Remove chicken and chop it up, discarding skin and bones.
- Return chicken to pot and pour in cream of chicken soup; heat with lid off, stirring to combine.
- Cook noodles separately according to package directions.
- Once noodles are cooked, drain and put into Instant Pot®.
- Season soup with salt and black pepper.

8. Vegan Chili (Vegetarian, Gluten-free, Family Friendly)

Prep Time: 10 minutes
Pressure: 20 minutes
Total: 35 minutes
Pressure Level: Low
Release: Quick
Per Serving: Calories: 192, Protein: 16g, Fat: 5g, Total Carbs: 25g, Fiber: 8g
Servings: 8

Ingredients:

- 2 tablespoons olive oil
- 2 yellow onions, chopped
- 1 teaspoon garlic, minced
- 1 (12 oz) package veggie ground round (such as Yves brand)
- 1 tablespoon chili powder
- 1 red bell pepper, diced
- 2 teaspoons cumin
- 1 teaspoon oregano
- Salt and pepper to taste
- 8 ounces pinto beans (soak before using)
- 8 ounces kidney beans (soak before using)
- 14 ounces Roma tomatoes, chopped

- 4 cups water

Directions:

- Heat oil in Instant Pot®; sauté onions and garlic.
- Add veggie ground round and brown.
- Add chili powder, bell pepper, cumin, oregano, salt and black pepper; mix well.
- Add beans, tomatoes and water; stir, blending well.
- Secure lid, set at low pressure and cook for 20 minutes.
- Carefully use quick release.

Chapter 4 - Instant Pot® Dinner Recipes
9. Meatballs with Marina Sauce (Family Friendly)

Prep Time: 30 minutes
Pressure: 5 minutes
Total: 40 minutes
Pressure Level: High
Release: Quick
Per Serving: Calories: 550, Protein: 38g, Fat: 24g, Total Carbs: 55g, Fiber: 15g
Servings: 4

Ingredients:

- 2 tablespoons olive oil
- 1 onion, diced
- 2 teaspoons garlic, minced
- ¼ cup red pepper flakes
- 2 teaspoons oregano
- 2 cans (14.5 oz each) tomatoes, crushed
- ½ cup breadcrumbs
- ¼ cup milk
- ½ pound each lean ground beef and ground pork, mixed together
- 3 tablespoons parsley, minced

- 1 large egg
- ½ cup Parmesan cheese, grated
- Salt and pepper to taste
- Fresh basil, chopped, for garnish

Directions:

- Heat oil in Instant Pot®; sauté onion for 5 minutes.
- Add garlic, red pepper flakes, and oregano; sauté for an additional 30 seconds.
- Add crushed tomatoes; reduce heat and simmer for 10 minutes.
- Mix breadcrumbs and milk in medium bowl.
- Mix in meat, parsley, egg, cheese, salt and pepper; form into balls.
- Add to pressure cooker. Secure lid; set at high pressure and cook for 5 minutes.
- Carefully use quick release; garnish with basil.

10. Miso Risotto (Low-Carb, Vegetarian, Family Friendly)

Prep Time: 20 minutes
Pressure: 10 minutes
Total: 35 minutes
Pressure Level: Low
Release: Quick
Per Serving: Calories: 568, Protein: 7g, Fat: 22g, Total Carbs: 79g, Fiber: 1g
Servings: 6

Ingredients:

- 6 tablespoons olive oil
- 1 teaspoon garlic, minced
- 1 shallot, minced
- 2 cups Arborio rice
- ½ cup saké
- ¼ cup white miso paste
- 2 teaspoons soy sauce

- 4 cups of vegetable stock, low-sodium
- ½ teaspoon lemon juice
- Salt to taste
- Minced scallions

Directions:

- Heat oil in Instant Pot®; sauté garlic and shallot.
- Add in rice; stir until toasted, but not browned (about 4 minutes).
- Pour in saké, stirring until evaporated.
- Add miso and soy sauce; mix well. Deglaze pot with vegetable stock.
- Secure lid, set at low pressure and cook for 5 minutes. Use quick release.
- Add lemon juice; stir well.
- Season with salt; sprinkle with chopped scallions.

11. Black-Eyed Peas & Collard Green Chili (Vegetarian, Family Friendly)

Prep Time: 15 minutes
Pressure: 10 minutes
Total: 30 minutes
Pressure Level: High
Release: Naturally
Per Serving: Calories: 194, Protein: 6g, Fat: 1.2g, Total Carbs: 42g, Fiber: 11g
Servings: 6

Ingredients:

- 4 large collard green leaves
- 1 teaspoon olive oil
- 2 teaspoons minced garlic
- 1 cup diced onion
- 2 cups chopped celery
- 2 cups chopped carrots
- 1 teaspoon ground cumin
- 2 tablespoons chili powder
- ½ teaspoon ground coriander
- 1 tablespoon oregano

- 1 teaspoon cinnamon
- 1 fresh jalapeno, seeded and diced
- 1 cup water
- 2 cups dried black-eyed peas
- 2 bay leaves
- 1 can (8 ounces) tomato sauce
- 1 can (28 ounces) diced tomatoes
- 2 cups vegetable broth, low-sodium
- Green onion, chopped for garnish
- Sea salt to taste

Directions:

- Cut collard greens lengthwise and remove inner ribs; cut crosswise into strips about 6mm wide; set aside.
- Heat oil in Instant Pot®; sauté garlic and onions for a few minutes.
- Add celery and carrots, cooking for 5 minutes.
- Add cumin, collard greens, chili powder, coriander, oregano, cinnamon and jalapeno; sauté for about 1 minute.
- Add water, black-eyed peas, bay leaves, tomato sauce, tomatoes, and broth. Secure lid, set at high pressure and cook for 10 minutes.
- Decrease pressure naturally.
- Remove bay leaves before serving.

12. Vegan Hot Tamales (Vegetarian, Family Friendly)

Prep Time: 50 minutes
Pressure: 20 minutes
Total: 1 hour and 10 minutes
Pressure Level: High
Release: Naturally
Per Serving: Calories: 123, Protein: 1.4g, Fat: 10g, Total Carbs: 8.3g, Fiber: .7g
Servings: 15

Ingredients:

- 1 pack corn husks
- 3 cups masa harina
- 1 cup corn oil
- 2 teaspoons baking powder
- 1 teaspoon sea salt

Fillings:

- 2 cups rice
- 3 cans refried beans
- 2 cups salsa
- Chili sauce
- 2 cups water

Directions:

- Rinse corn husks and arrange in casserole dish; cover with boiling water (place another dish over top to keep husks submerged).
- In mixer combine masa harina, baking powder and salt.
- Add oil and mix until dough is consistency of Play-doh.
- Construct tamales as follows: Flip the husks so the side that was down in the casserole dish is now facing up.
- Dry with paper towel.
- Spread layer of masa mixture in middle 2/3 of husk.
- Add a dollop of your choice of filling in the middle; top with chili sauce.
- Fold in sides, then fold bottom up; leave top open.
- Add 2 cups of water to Instant Pot®.
- Add steamer basket.
- Put tamales in steamer basket. Secure lid, set at high pressure and cook for 15 minutes.
- Let pressure release naturally.

13. Barbeque Sausage (Family Friendly)

Prep Time: 22 minutes
Pressure: 10 minutes
Total: 35 minutes
Pressure Level: High
Release: Quick
Per Serving: Calories: 157, Protein: 6g, Fat: 10g, Carbs: 8g, Fiber: 0
Servings: 4-6

Ingredients:

- 2 pounds smoked sausage
- ½ cup barbeque sauce
- ½ tablespoon brown sugar
- ½ tablespoon lemon juice

Directions:

- Cut sausage into 1-inch pieces; place sausage bites into Instant Pot®.
- Add in enough water to cover meat. Secure lid; set at high pressure and cook for 10 minutes. Drain.
- Stir together barbecue sauce, sugar and lemon juice; pour over sausage and serve with toothpicks.

14. Creole Cod (Family Friendly, Low-Carb)

Prep Time: 5 minutes
Pressure: 15 minutes
Total: 20 minutes
Pressure Level: High
Release: Quick
Per Serving: Calories: 350, Protein: 52g, Fat: 11g, Total Carbs: 6g, Fiber: 0g
Servings: 8

Ingredients:

- ¼ cup olive oil
- 1 cup celery, chopped
- 1 green pepper, chopped
- 2 cups white onion, chopped
- 1 teaspoon minced garlic
- 1 can (28-oz) tomatoes
- ¼ cup white wine
- 2 pounds frozen cod fillets
- 2 bay leaves
- 1 tablespoon paprika
- ½ teaspoon cayenne pepper
- Sea salt to taste

Directions:

- Heat oil in Instant Pot®; sauté celery, green pepper, onion, and garlic.
- Remove veggies and place on plate.
- Drain juice from a can of tomatoes.
- Pour the tomato juice and wine into the Instant Pot®.
- Place fish in a steamer basket in a crisscross fashion.
- Put into the Instant Pot®. Secure lid, set at high pressure and cook for 5 minutes. Use quick release.
- Remove fish; add veggies, tomatoes, bay leaves, paprika, cayenne pepper and salt to liquid in pot.
- Place fish back into pot, secure lid and cook at high pressure for 10 more minutes.
- Release heat using quick release.

15. Turkey & Veggie Soup (Family Friendly)

Prep Time: 90 minutes
Pressure: 50 minutes
Total: 100 minutes
Pressure Level: High
Release: Naturally
Per Serving: Calories: 73, Protein: 4g, Fat: 3g, Total Carbs: 8.3g, Fiber: .6
Servings: 8

Broth Ingredients:

- Turkey bones with meat on them
- 1 stalk celery, chopped
- 2 bay leaves
- 1 carrot, sliced
- 1 onion, diced
- ½ teaspoon salt
- 3 quarts water

Soup Ingredients:

- 1 tablespoon butter

- 1 minced shallot
- 1 teaspoon fresh thyme
- 2 quarts turkey stock
- 2 cups shredded turkey
- 2 cups frozen mixed veggies
- 1 ½ cups egg noodles
- Salt and pepper to taste

Directions:

- To make the broth: place turkey bones, celery, bay leaves, carrot, onion, and salt in pressure cooker.
- Pour in water, secure lid, set at high pressure and cook for 50 minutes.
- Let pressure release naturally.
- Remove solids. Use 2 quarts of this stock for soup:
- Melt some butter in Instant Pot®. Sauté the shallot with thyme until browned.
- Add in 2 quarts of turkey stock. Bring to a boil.
- Add in the turkey meat and mixed veggies along with noodles.
- Salt and pepper to taste. Simmer for 10 minutes or until heated through.

16.French Onion Soup (Family Friendly)

Prep Time: 10 minutes
Pressure: 8 minutes
Total: 35 minutes
Pressure Level: High
Release: Quick
Per Serving: Calories: 194, Protein: 8g, Fat: 8g, Total Carbs: 15g, Fiber: 1g
Servings: 5

Ingredients:

- 1 tablespoon olive oil
- 4 cups diced sweet onion
- 2 teaspoons minced garlic
- ½ cup dry sherry
- 4 cups beef broth, low-sodium
- 2 teaspoons dried thyme
- Salt and pepper to taste
- ½ cup shredded Gruyere cheese

- 5 slices French baguette (optional)

Directions:

- Heat olive oil in Instant Pot®; add onions and garlic, sautéing until soft.
- Add cooking sherry, 2 cups of broth and thyme. Secure lid, set at high pressure and cook for 8 minutes. Use quick release.
- Add rest of broth and simmer, seasoning with salt and pepper as desired.
- Pour soup into oven-proof bowls; add slice of baguette to each bowl, sprinkle cheese on top, and broil in oven for 3 minutes or until cheese is melted.

17. Chicken Wild Rice Soup (Family Friendly)

Prep Time: 15 minutes
Pressure: 30 minutes
Total: 45 minutes
Pressure Level: High
Release: Quick
Per Serving: Calories: 380, Protein: 19g, Fat: 21g, Total Carbs: 23g, Fiber: 2g
Servings: 4

Ingredients:

- ½ cup wild rice
- 4 cups chicken stock
- 1 large chicken breast, skinless, boneless, cubed
- 4 carrots, diced
- 2 celery stalks, diced
- 1 onion, diced
- 2 tablespoons almond flour
- 2 tablespoons butter
- 6 ounces sliced mushrooms

- 1 cup of heavy whipping cream
- Salt, pepper and nutmeg to taste

Directions:

- Add wild rice and chicken stock to the Instant Pot®. Secure lid, set at high pressure and cook for 20 minutes.
- Use quick release. Add in chicken, carrots, celery, and onion. Secure lid, set at high pressure and cook for an additional 3 minutes.
- In a mixing bowl, blend flour and butter; add in sherry and mushrooms.
- Add mixture to the Instant Pot® and cook uncovered for 5 minutes.
- Add heavy whipping cream and mix thoroughly.
- Season with salt, pepper and nutmeg; enjoy!

18.Bourbon Chicken Wings (Low-Carb)

Prep Time: 10 minutes
Pressure: 10 minutes
Total: 30 minutes
Pressure Level: High
Release: Quick
Per Serving: Calories: 239, Protein: 20g, Fat: 15g, Total Carbs: 8g, Fiber: 0
Servings: 2-4

Ingredients:

- 2 tablespoons olive oil
- 2 pounds chicken wings
- 1 cup barbecue sauce
- ¼ cup bourbon
- 1 tablespoon honey
- ¾ cups water
- 1 tablespoon brown sugar
- 2 teaspoons paprika
- 2 teaspoons liquid smoke
- ¼ teaspoon cayenne
- Salt and pepper to taste

Directions:

- Add olive oil to Instant Pot®; add wings and sauté for 10 minutes, browning on both sides.
- Place remaining ingredients in small bowl and mix well.
- Add mixture to wings in Instant Pot® and coat well.
- Secure lid; set at high pressure and cook for 10 minutes. Use quick release.

19. Pot Roast (Family Friendly)

Prep Time: 30 minutes
Pressure: 1 hour
Total: 1 hour and 35 minutes
Pressure Level: High
Release: Naturally
Per Serving: Calories: 467.6, Protein: 37g, Fat: 22g, Carbs: 30.4g, Fiber: 4.3g
Servings: 4

Ingredients:

- 3 ½ pounds beef chuck or rump roast
- 1 tablespoon olive oil
- 1 yellow onion, chopped
- 2 bay leaves
- 1 ½ cups beef broth, low-sodium
- 1 tablespoon cornstarch

Directions:

- Pat roast dry and add seasonings.
- Heat olive oil in Instant Pot®; brown meat on both sides.
- Remove meat; sauté onions; add bay leaves and beef broth.
- Add meat to pot, secure lid, set at high pressure and cook for 1 hour.

- Turn off heat and allow pressure to release naturally.
- Plate the roast, and allow to rest.
- Thicken juices in pot with cornstarch to make gravy.
- Pour gravy over roast and serve with potatoes or mixed veggies.

20. Corned Beef & Cabbage (Family Friendly)

Prep Time: 10 minutes
Pressure: 90 minutes
Total: 110 minutes
Pressure Level: High
Release: Quick
Per Serving: Calories: 302, Protein: 18g, Fat: 16.3g, Carbs: 22g, Fiber: 3.5g
Servings: 6

Ingredients:

- 3 pounds flat-cut corned beef brisket
- 4 cups of beef broth, low-sodium
- 2 teaspoons minced garlic
- 1 package corned beef seasoning
- 1 onion, cut into wedges
- 6 red potatoes, quartered
- 3 carrots, cut into small pieces
- 1 small cabbage, cut into 6 wedges

Directions:

- Rinse corned beef. Add broth, garlic, seasoning and onion to Instant Pot®.

- Place corned beef on rack attachment and lower into pot. Secure lid, set at high pressure and cook for 90 minutes.
- Use quick release; remove the rack and beef from pot.
- Add veggies to pot; secure lid, set at high pressure and cook for 3 minutes.
- Use quick release; serve and enjoy!

21. Mongolian Beef (Family Friendly)

Prep Time: 10 minutes
Pressure: 12 minutes
Total: 25 minutes
Pressure Level: High
Release: Quick
Per Serving: Calories: 359, Protein: 18g, Fat: 13g, Carbs: 43g, Fiber: 0g
Servings: 6

Ingredients:

- 2 pounds flank steak
- Salt and pepper to taste
- 1 tablespoon olive oil
- 1 teaspoon garlic, minced
- ½ cup soy sauce, low-sodium
- ½ cup water
- ½ teaspoon minced ginger
- 2/3 cup dark brown sugar
- 2 tablespoons cornstarch
- 3 tablespoons water
- 3 green onions, sliced into 1-inch pieces

Directions:

- Season beef with salt and pepper. Heat olive oil in Instant Pot® and brown the meat.
- Remove meat once browned.
- Add garlic to pot and sauté.
- Add soy sauce, half cup of water, ginger, and brown sugar to pot.
- Add beef back to pot. Secure lid, set at high pressure and cook for 12 minutes. Use quick release.
- Mix cornstarch and 3 tablespoons of water in a bowl; add to pot and bring to boil.
- Mix in the green onions; serve with rice and veggies.

22. Beef Stroganoff (Family Friendly)

Prep Time: 10 minutes
Pressure: 18 minutes
Total: 45 minutes
Pressure Level: High
Release: Quick
Per Serving: Calories: 334, Protein: 28g, Fat: 17.4g, Carbs: 21.6g, Fiber: 0
Servings: 6

Ingredients:

- 1 ½ pounds lean beef, cut into 1-inch chunks
- 1 tablespoon olive oil
- 1 yellow onion, chopped
- 1 cup dry white wine
- 1 tablespoon almond flour
- 1 tablespoon Dijon mustard
- 1 cup beef broth, low-sodium
- 1 pound button mushrooms, sliced

- 2 sticks celery, chopped
- 3 carrots, chopped
- ¼ cup Neufchatel cheese
- ¼ cup parsley, chopped
- Salt and pepper to taste
- 10 ounces whole-wheat egg noodles

Directions:
- Season beef with salt and pepper; heat olive oil in Instant Pot®, add beef, and brown on all sides.
- Add in onions, and stir. Mix in white wine, flour, and mustard; simmer for a few minutes. Pour in broth; add mushrooms, celery and carrots. Secure lid, set at high pressure and cook for 18 minutes.
- Use quick release; add cheese, parsley, salt and pepper.
- In separate pot, prepare egg noodles according to package instructions.
- Serve beef on bed of egg noodles.

23. Chicken Cacciatore (Low-Carb)

Prep Time: 12 minutes
Pressure: 12 minutes
Total: 30 minutes
Pressure Level: high
Release: Quick
Per Serving: Calories: 238, Protein: 32g, Fat: 5g, Carbs: 10, Fiber: 2.3g
Servings: 3

Ingredients:

- 2 tablespoons olive oil
- 2 pounds chicken thighs, boneless, skinless
- Salt and pepper to taste
- 1 white onion, minced
- 1 teaspoon minced garlic
- ¼ teaspoon red pepper flakes
- 1 teaspoon oregano
- 1 bay leaf
- ¼ cup chicken broth
- 1 can (28-ounce) diced tomatoes
- 2 green bell peppers, diced

Directions:

- Heat olive oil in Instant Pot®. Season chicken with salt and pepper; brown in oil and remove to plate.
- Add onion to pot and sauté for about 5 minutes; add garlic, red pepper flakes and oregano.
- Add bay leaf, broth and tomatoes; return chicken to pot. Secure lid, set at high pressure and cook for 10 minutes. Use quick release.
- Add green peppers, secure lid, and bring to high pressure again for 2 minutes. Use quick release; remove bay leaf.
- Serve over rice or pasta.

24.   Lime-Salsa Mozzarella Chicken (Family Friendly, Low-Carb)

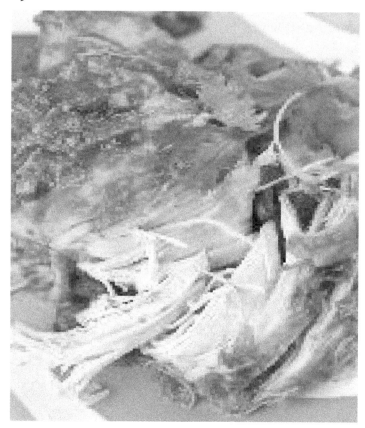

Prep Time: 15 minutes
Pressure: 12 minutes
Total: 32 minutes
Pressure Level: High
Release: Quick
Per Serving: Calories: 294, Protein: 34g, Fat: 5g, Carbs: 9g, Fiber: 0g
Servings: 4

Ingredients:

- 4 chicken breasts, skinless, boneless
- 1 cup tomato sauce
- 1 cup salsa
- juice of 2 limes
- ½ teaspoon salt
- ¼ teaspoon pepper
- 1 cup grated Mozzarella cheese

Directions:

- Add chicken to Instant Pot® along with sauce, salsa, lime juice, salt and pepper. Secure lid, set at high pressure and cook for 12 minutes.
- Use quick release. Remove chicken and place in oven-proof dish.
- Cook sauce a little longer in pot, then spoon over chicken and top with cheese.
- Place under broiler for 5 minutes; serve with Mexican rice or veggies.

25. Thai Peanut Chicken Thighs (Low-Carb)

Prep Time: 5 minutes
Pressure: 12 minutes
Total: 20 minutes
Pressure Level: High
Release: Quick
Per Serving: Calories: 365, Protein: 35.2g, Fat: 20.1g, Carbs: 7.5g, Fiber: 2.1g
Servings: 4-6

Ingredients:

- 1 tablespoon olive oil
- 8 chicken thighs, skinless, boneless
- ½ cup chicken broth, low-sodium
- 1 tablespoon dried cilantro
- ¼ cup soy sauce
- ¼ cup natural peanut butter
- 1 teaspoon red pepper flakes
- 1 tablespoon ground ginger
- 2 tablespoons lime juice
- 1 tablespoon cornstarch

- 2 tablespoons water
- ¼ cup unsalted peanuts, chopped
- 3 chopped green onions, for garnish
- Salt and pepper to taste

Directions:

- Heat olive oil in Instant Pot® using 'browning' setting.
- Brown chicken; set aside on plate.
- Mix broth, cilantro, soy sauce, peanut butter, red pepper flakes, ginger and lime juice in pot.
- Add chicken back to the pot. Secure lid, set at high pressure and cook for 12 minutes.
- Use quick release. Whisk cornstarch and water in a bowl, add to cooker, mix well and serve.
- Garnish with peanuts and green onions.

26. Beef Ribs (Family Friendly)

Prep Time: 15 minutes
Pressure: 60 minutes
Total: 80 minutes
Pressure Level: Low
Release: Naturally
Per Serving: Calories: 400, Protein: 25g, Fat: 21g, Carbs: 23g, Fiber: 1g
Servings: 4

Ingredients:

- 1 teaspoon minced garlic
- 1 tablespoon sesame oil
- 1 piece of ginger, chopped
- dash red pepper flakes
- 2/3 cup soy sauce
- ¼ cup rice vinegar
- 1/3 cup sugar
- 2/3 cup beef stock, low-sodium
- 8 beef ribs, cut in half
- 2 tablespoons cornstarch
- 4 tablespoons water

Directions:

- Sauté garlic, sesame oil, ginger, and red pepper flakes in Instant Pot®.
- Add in soy sauce, vinegar, sugar and beef stock.
- Add in ribs, turning to coat. Secure lid, set at low pressure and cook for 60 minutes.
- Remove from heat; allow pressure to release naturally.
- Remove ribs from pot and place in shallow pan; place under broiler for 5 minutes.
- Mix cornstarch and water in small bowl; add to liquid in pot and boil. Pour over ribs and serve.

27. Shredded Flank Pepper Steak (Family Friendly, Low-Carb)

Prep Time: 10 minutes
Pressure: 20 minutes
Total: 30 minutes
Pressure Level: High
Release: Quick
Per Serving: Calories: 448, Protein: 56g, Fat: 22g, Carbs: 2g, Fiber: 0g
Servings: 4

Ingredients:

- 2 pounds flank steak
- Dash of sea salt
- 1 cup chicken broth, low-sodium
- 2 teaspoons minced garlic
- 1 large onion, quartered
- Black pepper to taste

Directions:

- Season steak with salt. Add steak, broth, garlic and onion to Instant Pot®.
- Set at medium-high heat and bring to boil.
- Once boiling secure the lid, set at high pressure and cook for 20 minutes. Use quick release.
- Remove steak; shred and season with favorite seasonings.

28. Meatloaf (Family Friendly)

Prep Time: 10 minutes
Pressure: 15 minutes
Total: 30 minutes
Pressure Level: High
Release: Naturally, 10 minutes; Quick for remainder
Per Serving: Calories: 572, Protein: 53g, Fat: 26g, Carbs: 26g, Fiber: 2g
Servings: 6

Ingredients:

- 2 pounds lean ground beef
- ¼ cup grated Parmesan cheese
- ¼ onion, minced
- 1 egg, beaten
- 1 tablespoon minced garlic
- ½ cup breadcrumbs
- 2 teaspoons Worcestershire sauce
- 1 teaspoon salt

- ½ teaspoon black pepper
- ½ teaspoon thyme
- 1 tablespoon olive oil
- 1 yellow onion, diced
- ½ cup broth
- 1 cup ketchup

Directions:

- In mixing bowl mix beef, cheese, minced onion, egg, garlic, breadcrumbs, Worcestershire, salt, pepper, and thyme; form into loaf with hands.
- Heat oil in Instant Pot®; sauté diced onion.
- Add stock and ketchup; stir to combine.
- Place meatloaf into pot. Secure lid, set at high pressure and cook for 15 minutes.
- Allow pressure to release naturally for 10 minutes, then quick release.

29. Coconut Fish Curry (Family Friendly, Low-Carb)

Prep Time: 5 minutes
Pressure: 5 minutes
Total: 15 minutes
Pressure Level: Low
Release: Quick
Per Serving: Calories: 172, Protein: 26g, Fat: 4g, Carbs: 8g, Fiber: 2g
Servings: 8

Ingredients:

- 4 basil leaves
- 1 tablespoon grated ginger
- 1 teaspoon minced garlic
- 2 white onions, cut into strips
- 2 tablespoons ground cumin
- ½ teaspoon ground turmeric
- ½ teaspoon ground fenugreek
- 1 teaspoon chili powder
- 1 tablespoon ground coriander
- 2 cups unsweetened coconut milk
- 2 pounds white fish, cut into bite-size pieces
- 1 tomato, chopped

- 2 bell peppers, cut into strips
- Dash lemon juice

Directions:

- Heat oil in Instant Pot®; sauté basil leaves, ginger, garlic, and onion.
- Add in cumin, turmeric, fenugreek, chili and coriander; saute for 2 minutes.
- Add coconut milk and fish along with tomato and peppers. Secure lid, set at low pressure and cook for 5 minutes.
- Use quick release; serve with dash of lemon juice.

30. Mussels (Family Friendly)

Prep Time: 5 minutes
Pressure: 1 minute
Total: 8 minutes
Pressure Level: Low
Release: Quick
Per Serving: Calories: 302, Protein: 32g, Fat: 4g, Carbs: 16g, Fiber: 0g
Servings: 3

Ingredients:

- 2 pounds mussels
- 1 tablespoon olive oil
- 1 white onion, chopped
- ½ teaspoon minced garlic
- ½ cup water
- ½ cup white wine
- 1 package baby spinach
- 1 head radicchio, cut into thin strips

Directions:

- Scrub mussel shells and remove beard. Heat olive oil in Instant Pot®.
- Add in onion, garlic, water and wine.

- Add mussels to steamer basket and place into pot. Secure lid, set at low pressure and cook for 1 minute.
- Use quick release. Create a bed of baby spinach and radicchio strips in a bowl; add mussels and pour broth over.

31.   Salmon Risotto (Low-Fat)

Prep Time: 10 minutes
Pressure: 6 minutes
Total: 22 minutes
Pressure Level: High
Release: Quick
Per Serving: Calories: 412, Protein: 29g, Fat: 3g, Carbs: 60g, Fiber: 5g
Servings: 4

Ingredients:

- 1 teaspoon olive oil
- 1 yellow onion, chopped
- 2 cups Arborio rice
- ½ cup white wine
- ¾ cup water
- 2 cans chicken broth, low-sodium
- Salt and pepper to taste
- 1 cup frozen peas
- 1 pound skinless salmon fillets
- 1½ teaspoons grated lemon peel

Directions:

- Heat oil in Instant Pot®; add onion and sauté for about 5 minutes.
- Add rice and stir for 2 minutes.
- Add wine and cook for 30 seconds, until wine has evaporated.
- Add water, broth, salt and pepper. Secure lid, set at high pressure and cook for 6 minutes. Use quick release.
- Remove lid, add peas and salmon, top with lemon peel. Cover and let stand for 5 minutes.
- The salmon will cook in the still-hot pot.

32. Clam Chowder (Low-Fat)

Prep Time: 8 minutes
Pressure: 5 minutes
Total: 15 minutes
Pressure Level: High
Release: Quick
Per Serving: Calories: 264, Protein: 14g, Fat: 10g, Carbs: 17g, Fiber: 5g
Servings: 6

Ingredients:

- 1 cup smoked bacon
- 1 yellow onion, finely chopped
- Pinch red pepper flakes
- Salt to taste
- ½ cup white wine
- 2 potatoes, skin on, cubed
- 2 cups clam juice
- 1 bay leaf
- 1 sprig thyme
- Dash cayenne pepper
- 1 tablespoon flour
- 1 tablespoon butter

- 24 fresh clams
- 1 cup cream
- 1 cup milk

Directions:

- Add bacon to Instant Pot®; cook until fat coats bottom of pot.
- Add onion, pepper, and salt; sauté.
- Add wine; cook until evaporated, add potatoes and mix well.
- Add clam juice, bay leaf, thyme and dash of cayenne pepper. Secure lid, set at high pressure and cook for 5 minutes.
- While this cooks, prepare roux by stirring butter and flour together in skillet over low heat.
- Use quick release; add clams, cream, roux, and milk, stirring to combine.
- Simmer for 5 minutes and serve.

33. Ramen (Family Friendly)

Prep Time: 10 minutes
Pressure: 90 minutes
Total: 110 minutes
Pressure Level: High
Release: Naturally
Per Serving: Calories: 551, Protein: 16g, Fat: 18g, Carbs: 72g, Fiber: 2g
Servings: 8

Ingredients:

- 1½ pounds chicken wings
- 2½ pounds pork spareribs, cut into 2-inch pieces
- 2 tablespoons olive oil
- 2 small onions, sliced
- 1 teaspoon minced garlic
- Small piece ginger, grated
- Water
- Soy sauce, low-sodium, to taste
- 8 cups Chinese wheat noodles, cooked

Optional toppings: cooked bamboo shoots, seaweed, sesame seeds, minced scallions, bean sprouts

Directions:

- Boil water in a stockpot; add ribs and wings and allow to boil for 8 minutes.
- Remove meat and discard water; rinse meat.
- Heat oil in Instant Pot®; sauté onions, garlic, and ginger.
- Add meat; fill with water to max line. Secure lid, set at high pressure and cook for 90 minutes.
- Release pressure naturally.
- Strain out solids and discard.
- Add soy sauce and optional toppings of choice to the remaining rich, dark broth.
- Add 1 cup of cooked noodles to each serving bowl, top with broth and enjoy.

34. Teriyaki Salmon (Family Friendly)

Prep Time: 5 minutes
Pressure: 4 minutes
Total: 15 minutes
Pressure Level: High
Release: Quick
Per Serving: Calories 390, Protein: 31g, Fat: 20g, Carbs: 20g, Fiber: 0g
Servings: 4

Ingredients:

- 1½ cups boiling water
- 2 ounces dried mushrooms
- 4 Bok Choy leaves, cut in half, washed
- 3 spring onions, cut in half

- 2 tablespoons sweet rice wine
- 1 teaspoon sugar
- 1 teaspoon sesame oil
- 4 pieces fresh salmon

Directions:

- Place dried mushrooms in a bowl and carefully pour boiling water over them.
- Place Bok Choy in Instant Pot® and add next 4 ingredients (as well as mushrooms and water) to pot; layer salmon on top. Secure lid, set at high pressure and cook for 4 minutes.
- Use quick release, and serve.

35. Chicken, Chorizo & Kale Soup (Family Friendly)

Prep Time: 15 minutes
Pressure: 4 minutes
Total: 20 minutes
Pressure Level: High
Release: Quick
Per Serving: Calories: 329, Protein: 17g, Fat: 19g, Carbs: 15g, Fiber: 3g
Servings: 8

Ingredients:

- 2 tablespoons olive oil
- 4 chicken thighs, boneless, skinless, diced
- 9 ounces pork chorizo, casing removed
- 2 onions, chopped
- 2 teaspoons minced garlic
- 2 bay leaves
- 4 cups chicken broth, low-sodium
- 1 can (15 ounces) diced tomatoes
- 3 Yukon Gold potatoes, peeled and diced

- 5 ounces baby kale
- 1 can (15 ounces) chickpeas, drained and rinsed
- Salt and pepper to taste

Directions:

- Heat olive oil in Instant Pot®; add chicken and chorizo, along with onion, and sauté for 5 minutes.
- Add garlic, stirring to combine.
- Add bay leaves, broth and tomatoes, mixing well.
- Add potatoes and kale. Secure lid, and set at high pressure and cook for 4 minutes. Use quick release.
- Discard bay leaves; add in chickpeas. Salt and pepper to taste.

36. Creamy Butternut Squash and Ginger Soup (Low-Carb)

Prep Time: 12 minutes
Pressure: 15 minutes
Total: 35 minutes
Pressure Level: High
Release: Quick
Per Serving: Calories: 396, Protein: 17g, Fat: 7g, Carbs: 6g, Fiber: 2g
Servings: 4

Ingredients

- 1 tablespoon olive oil
- 1 onion, chopped
- 1 sprig sage
- Salt and pepper to taste
- 4 pounds butternut squash, seeded, peeled and cubed
- 2-inch piece fresh ginger, peeled, sliced
- 4 cups vegetable stock
- ¼ teaspoon nutmeg

Directions:

- Place oil in Instant Pot® and sauté onions and sage seasoned with salt and pepper.
- Once onions are softened, add enough squash to cover the bottom of the pot; stir and brown for 10 minutes.
- Add in remainder of squash, ginger, stock and nutmeg. Secure the lid, set at high pressure and cook for 15 minutes.
- Use quick release; remove sage stem.
- Blend into a soup with immersion blender. (If using regular blender, be very careful with hot liquids!) Serve and enjoy!

37. Seafood Gumbo (Family Friendly)

Prep Time: 20 minutes
Pressure: 10 minutes
Total: 35 minutes
Pressure Level: High
Release: Naturally
Per Serving: Calories: 823, Protein: 35g, Fat: 56g, Carbs: 33g, Fiber: 1g
Servings: 10

Ingredients:

- ¾ cup vegetable oil
- 1 cup white flour
- 2 tablespoons peanut oil
- 1¼ cup diced celery
- 1 cup diced green bell pepper
- 1 teaspoon minced garlic
- 1 cup diced white onion

- 3 bay leaves
- 1 teaspoon cayenne pepper
- ½ teaspoon onion powder
- 1 teaspoon celery seeds
- 1 teaspoon paprika
- salt and pepper to taste
- 2 quarts chicken stock, low-sodium
- 1 pound hot Italian sausage
- 6 plum tomatoes, peeled, seeded, diced
- Half a lump crab meat
- 2 dozen oysters, shucked
- 2 dozen cooked crawfish tails

Directions:

- To make the roux, combine the vegetable oil and flour in a skillet over medium heat.
- Keep stirring until it turns a dark brown color and has a nutty smell; be careful not to let it burn!
- Place peanut oil in Instant Pot®; add celery, bell pepper, garlic, and onion, turning to coat, and sauté for about 15 minutes.
- Add in spices, chicken stock, sausage and tomatoes.
- Slowly add in prepared roux until desired thickness is achieved; add seafood. Secure lid, set at high pressure and cook for 10 minutes.
- Reduce pressure naturally.

38. Tomato Basil Soup (Family Friendly)

Prep Time: 5 minutes
Pressure: 5 minutes
Total: 20 minutes
Pressure Level: High
Release: Quick
Per Serving: Calories: 312, Protein: 10g, Fat: 22g, Carbs: 15g, Fiber: 2g
Servings: 8

Ingredients:

- 3 tablespoons butter
- 1 carrot, diced
- 1 yellow onion, diced
- 2 celery stalks, diced
- 1 teaspoon minced garlic
- 2 cans (14.5 ounces) chicken broth, low-sodium
- 3 pounds tomatoes, cored, peeled, and cut into quarters
- 1 tablespoon tomato paste
- ½ cup chopped fresh basil
- Salt and pepper to taste
- 1 cup half-and-half

- ½ cup grated Parmesan cheese

Directions:

- Melt butter in Instant Pot®. Sauté carrots, onions and celery until tender; add garlic and cook additional minute.
- Add chicken broth, tomatoes, paste, basil, salt and pepper. Secure lid, set at high pressure and cook for 5 minutes. Use quick release.
- Carefully puree soup in a blender until smooth.
- Stir in half-and-half and cheese.

39. Vegan Feijoada (Vegetarian, Family Friendly)

Prep Time: 8 minutes
Pressure: 30 minutes
Total: 50 minutes
Pressure Level: High
Release: Naturally
Per Serving: Calories: 322, Protein: 19g, Fat: 3g, Carbs: 53g, Fiber: 12g
Servings: 6

Ingredients:

- 2 tablespoons oil
- 1 red bell pepper, chopped
- 2 teaspoons minced garlic
- 2 onions, sliced into rings
- 2 large carrots, cut into ¼-inch discs
- 1 tablespoon cumin
- ½ tablespoon liquid smoke
- Fresh ground pepper to taste
- ½ tablespoon paprika
- ½ tablespoon dried thyme
- 1/3 cup dry red wine
- 2 bay leaves

- 1 spicy vegan sausage, chopped
- 2 ½ cups water
- 2 cups dried black beans, soaked overnight
- 1 cup soy curls, softened in hot water for 15 minutes, drained

Optional toppings: avocado, onions, and cilantro

Directions:

- Sauté bell pepper, garlic, onions, and carrots in Instant Pot® for 5 minutes.
- Add cumin, liquid smoke, pepper, paprika, and thyme; add red wine and stir to combine.
- Add bay leaves, vegan sausage, water, beans and soy curls. Secure lid, set at high pressure and cook for 30 minutes.
- Allow the pressure to decrease naturally.

40. Spicy Lentils (Vegetarian, Family Friendly)

Prep Time: 10 minutes
Pressure: 15 minutes
Total: 30 minutes
Pressure Level: High
Release: Naturally
Per Serving: Calories: 102, Protein: 5g, Fat: 2g, Carbs: 11g, Fiber: 4g
Servings: 6

Ingredients:

- 1 tablespoon olive oil
- 1 green pepper, chopped
- 1 celery stalk, chopped
- 1½ cups dry lentils
- 1½ cups chopped tomatoes
- 2 cups water
- 1 teaspoon curry powder
- 1 teaspoon sea salt

Directions:

- Heat oil in Instant Pot®; sauté green pepper and celery.
- When soft, add in lentils, chopped tomatoes, water, curry powder and sea salt; mix well. Secure lid, set at high pressure and cook for 15 minutes.
- Release pressure naturally.

41. Chicken & Butternut Squash Soup (Low-Carb)

Prep Time: 10 minutes
Setting: Poultry, 25 minutes
Total: 40 minutes
Release: Naturally
Per Serving: Calories: 728, Protein: 35.9g, Total Fat: 44.8g, Total Carbs: 53.5g, Cholesterol: 157mg, Sodium: 275mg, Potassium: 1865mg,
Servings: 4-6

Ingredients:

- 2 cartons butternut squash soup
- 1 pound chicken breast, skinless, boneless, cut into small pieces
- 1 yellow onion, sliced
- 15 ounces roasted red peppers
- 2 tablespoons finely chopped green chili
- 1 teaspoon garlic powder
- 1 tablespoon olive oil
- Salt and pepper to taste
- 2 cups water
- ½ cup heavy cream

Directions:

- Combine all ingredients in Instant Pot®, mixing well. Secure lid, set at 'poultry' setting and cook for 25 minutes.
- Allow pressure to release naturally.
- Serve with rice and cauliflower.

42. Lamb Curry with Peppercorn (Low-Carb)

Prep Time: 15 minutes
Setting: Meat, 50 Minutes
Total: 75 minutes
Release: Naturally
Per Serving: Calories: 3,486, Protein: 518.3g, Total Fat: 133.2g, Total Carbs: 15.5g, Cholesterol: 1633mg, Sodium: 8582mg, Potassium: 6529mg
Servings: 4

Ingredients:

- 4 pounds lamb chops, cut into 2-inch cubes
- ¾ teaspoon ground pepper
- ½ cup soy sauce
- 1 cup water
- 2 bay leaves
- 2 teaspoons peppercorns
- ½ cup vinegar
- 1 teaspoon minced garlic

Directions:

- Combine all ingredients with lamb and marinate in refrigerator overnight.
- Place lamb and marinade in Instant Pot®, set at 'meat' setting and cook for 50 minutes. Release pressure naturally.
- Serve and enjoy.

43. Creamy Beef, Chicken & Cabbage (Family Friendly)

Prep Time: 15 minutes
Setting: Meat, 30 minutes; Poultry, 25 minutes
Total: 70 minutes
Release: Naturally
Per Serving: Calories: 1,909, Protein: 294.1g, Total Fat: 65.7g, Total Carbs: 18.9g, Cholesterol: 876mg, Sodium: 1024mg, Potassium: 4830mg,
Servings: 8

Ingredients:

- 2 tablespoons tomato puree
- 2 pounds ground beef, cooked and browned
- ¼ teaspoon black pepper
- 1 tablespoon Worcestershire sauce
- Salt to taste
- ¼ cup water
- 1/8 teaspoon paprika
- 2 pounds chicken breast, skinless, boneless, cut into small pieces
- 1 red bell pepper, chopped

- ¼ cup cream cheese
- ¼ cabbage, chopped

Directions:

- Mix tomato puree with ground beef, black pepper, Worcestershire sauce, salt, water and paprika in Instant Pot®. Secure lid, set at 'meat' setting and cook for 30 minutes.
- Use quick release; add remaining ingredients and mix well. Secure lid, set at 'poultry' setting and cook for additional 25 minutes.
- Allow pressure to release naturally. Serve with side dish of cauliflower rice.

44. Mushroom Curry (Family Friendly)

Prep Time: 12 minutes
Setting: Stew, 15 minutes
Total: 35 minutes
Release: Quick
Per Serving: Calories: 560, Protein: 13.1g, Total Fat: 33.0g, Total Carbs: 61.7g, Cholesterol: 0mg, Sodium: 8391mg, Potassium: 1188mg
Servings: 6

Ingredients:

- 8 ounces Portobello mushrooms, chopped
- ¼ cup brown sugar
- 1 can (8 ounces) tomato sauce
- ¼ cup green pepper, sliced
- 2 tablespoons olive oil
- ¼ cup shredded cabbage
- ½ cup soy sauce, low-sodium
- 1 tablespoon toasted sesame seeds

Directions:

- Combine first 7 ingredients in Instant Pot®. Secure lid, set at 'stew' and cook for 15 minutes. Use quick release.
- Garnish with toasted sesame seeds and enjoy!

45. Spicy Pork (Low-Carb, Family Friendly)

Prep Time: 12 minutes
Setting: Meat, 50 minutes
Total: 70 minutes
Release: Naturally
Per Serving: Calories: 1,611, Protein: 144.1g, Total Fat: 97.7g, Total Carbs: 49.5g, Cholesterol: 408mg, Sodium: 468mg, Potassium: 4435mg
Servings: 4

Ingredients:

- 1 teaspoon almond oil
- 1 teaspoon minced garlic
- ½ cup diced onion
- 4 medium zucchini, finely chopped
- 4 boneless pork chops, thick cut
- ¼ cup minced fresh cilantro
- 1 tablespoon curry powder
- ¼ teaspoon cayenne pepper
- ½ teaspoon cumin
- 1 teaspoon garam masala
- 1 cup coconut milk

Directions:

- Place oil in Instant Pot® and sauté garlic and onion until they become fragrant.
- Add zucchini and pork chops.
- Blend next 5 ingredients in a bowl and pour into pot; pour coconut milk over all. Secure lid, set at 'meat' and cook for 50 minutes.
- Release pressure naturally.

46. Creamy Sesame Beef (Family Friendly)

Prep Time: 10 minutes
Setting: Meat, 50 minutes
Total: 70 minutes
Release: Naturally
Per Serving: Calories: 671, Protein: 65.7g, Total Fat: 15.9g, Total Carbs: 69.7g, Cholesterol: 152mg, Sodium: 8535mg, Potassium: 2047mg
Servings: 4

Ingredients:

- 2-3 pounds beef, cut into thin strips
- ¼ teaspoon hot sauce
- ¼ cup packed light brown sugar
- 1 teaspoon minced garlic
- 1 teaspoon lemon juice
- ⅛ teaspoon cayenne pepper

- ½ cup soy sauce, low-sodium
- 8 ounces tomato sauce
- Salt and pepper to taste
- ¼ cup heavy cream
- 1 red bell pepper, finely sliced
- 1 tablespoon toasted sesame seeds

Directions:

- Place first 11 ingredients in Instant Pot®; secure lid, set at 'meat' and cook for 50 minutes.
- Release pressure naturally. Garnish with sesame seeds.

47. BBQ-Flavored Pork (Low-Carb)

Prep Time: 12 minutes
Setting: Meat, 30 minutes
Total: 50 minutes
Release: Naturally
Per Serving: Calories: 4,134, Protein: 320.3g, Total Fat: 294.6g, Total Carbs: 28.8g, Cholesterol: 1225mg, Sodium: 1064mg, Potassium: 4682mg
Servings: 4

Ingredients:

- 3 pounds roasted pork shoulder
- 2 tablespoons balsamic vinegar
- 1 tablespoon bacon grease
- ½ teaspoon paprika
- ½ teaspoon chipotle powder
- 1 teaspoon hot sauce
- 1 tablespoon prepared yellow mustard
- ½ teaspoon onion powder
- Pinch ground ginger
- Dash coriander

- 3 tablespoons apple butter
- 1 teaspoon minced garlic
- Pinch allspice

Directions:

- Cut roasted pork into bite-size pieces, set aside.
- In a mixing bowl, combine remaining ingredients to make BBQ sauce.
- Dip pork pieces into sauce, coating evenly; place pork into Instant Pot®.
- Pour remaining sauce into pot. Secure lid, set at 'meat' and cook for 30 minutes.
- Release pressure naturally.

48. Cheesy Mushrooms and Chicken Cubes (Low-Carb)

Prep Time: 8 minutes
Setting: Poultry for 30 minutes
Total: 45 minutes
Release: Quick
Per Serving: Calories: 896, Protein: 42.8g, Total Fat: 79.3g, Total Carbs: 4.3g, Cholesterol: 239mg, Sodium: 1219mg, Potassium: 223mg
Servings: 3-4

Ingredients:

- 2 tablespoons butter
- 2 tablespoons chopped onions
- 16 Portobello mushrooms, chopped
- 4 chicken breasts, skinless, boneless, cut into cubes
- 1½ cups cheddar cheese, shredded
- 1 tablespoon chopped fresh parsley

Directions:

- Place butter, onion and mushrooms in Instant Pot® and sauté for 3 minutes.
- Add in the chicken, cheese and parsley; stir to combine. Secure lid, set at 'poultry' and cook for 30 minutes.
- Use quick release.

49. Creamy Cheese Beef (Low-Carb)

Prep Time: 10 minutes
Setting: Meat, 50 minutes
Total: 65 minutes
Release: Quick
Per Serving: Calories: 3,190, Protein: 450.6g, Total Fat: 129.5g, Total Carbs: 29.0g, Cholesterol: 1354mg, Sodium: 1956mg, Potassium: 5843mg
Servings: 4

Ingredients:

- 1 large onion, sliced
- 1 teaspoon minced garlic
- 1 tablespoon bacon grease
- 1 pounds ground beef
- 2 tablespoons Worcestershire sauce
- ¼ teaspoon black pepper
- 3 ounces shredded mozzarella cheese
- 2 ounces heavy cream
- 2 tablespoons lemon juice
- ¼ teaspoon ground coriander
- Salt and pepper to taste

- 1 teaspoon ginger powder
- 1 tablespoon prepared yellow mustard
- Dash hot sauce

Directions:

- Sauté onion, minced garlic and bacon grease in Instant Pot® for 3 minutes.
- Add ground beef and sauté for 5 minutes.
- In a mixing bowl, blend remaining ingredients and add to pot. Secure lid, set at 'meat' and cook for 50 minutes.
- Use quick release.

50. Multi-Meat Blend (Family Friendly)

Prep Time: 10 minutes
Setting: Meat, 50 minutes
Total: 70 minutes
Release: Quick
Per Serving: Calories: 3,190, Protein: 298.4g, Total Fat: 201.5g, Total Carbs: 36.9g, Cholesterol: 1853mg, Sodium: 2804mg, Potassium: 4497mg
Servings: 6-8

Ingredients:

- 4 tablespoons butter
- 1 teaspoon minced garlic
- 2 teaspoons minced ginger
- 1 onion, sliced
- ½ pound ground beef
- ½ pound chicken, minced
- ½ pound ground lamb
- ½ pound ground pork

- 1 red bell pepper, chopped
- 2 cups chicken broth, low-sodium
- 2 tablespoons tomato puree
- Salt and pepper to taste
- 4 eggs
- 2 cups heavy cream
- 1 teaspoon allspice

Directions:

- Place butter, garlic, ginger, and onion into Instant Pot® and sauté for 3 minutes.
- In a mixing bowl, add remaining ingredients and blend well.
- Pour mixture into pot. Secure lid, set at 'meat' and cook for 50 minutes.
- Use quick release.

Bonus Recipes!

51.   Cheesy Tuna (Low-Carb)

Prep Time: 5 minutes
Setting: Manual, 30 minutes
Total: 40 minutes
Release: Quick
Per Serving: Calories: 1,728, Protein: 24.9g, Total Fat: 160.0g, Total Carbs: 35.0g, Cholesterol: 484mg, Sodium: 2428mg, Potassium: 957mg
Servings: 4

Ingredients:

- 5 tablespoons butter
- 1 teaspoon minced garlic
- 1 teaspoon dried tarragon
- 2 small white onions, thinly sliced
- 1 can tuna, cut into small pieces
- 1½ teaspoons Herbs de Provence
- 1 teaspoon allspice

- 8 ounces cream cheese
- ½ cup dry white wine
- ½ cup vegetable broth, low-sodium
- 2 teaspoons fish sauce
- ½ cup heavy cream

Directions:

- Place 2 tablespoons butter in Instant Pot®; add garlic, tarragon, and onion. Sauté for 3 minutes.
- Add remaining ingredients to pot. Secure lid, set at 'manual' and cook for 30 minutes.
- Use quick release.

52. Mexican Lamb (Family Friendly)

Prep Time: 12 minutes
Setting: Meat, 50 minutes
Total: 70 minutes
Release: Quick
Per Serving: Calories: 2,830, Protein: 322.0g, Total Fat: 148.8g, Total Carbs: 41.3g, Cholesterol: 1054mg, Sodium: 6094mg, Potassium: 4838mg
Servings: 4

Ingredients:

- 2 ounces black olives, drained and sliced
- 16 ounces salsa
- 1 teaspoon minced garlic
- ½ cup finely chopped onion
- Salt and pepper to taste
- 2 pounds lamb, boneless, cut into small pieces
- 1 cup beef stock, low-sodium
- 2 cups shredded cheddar cheese

Directions:

- Combine first 5 ingredients to create marinade; add lamb pieces and marinate overnight in refrigerator.
- Place marinated lamb in Instant Pot®; pour beef stock over meat. Secure lid, set at 'meat' and cook for 50 minutes.
- Use quick release; sprinkle with cheese and serve.

53. Continental Chicken (Low-Carb)

Prep Time: 12 minutes
Setting: Poultry, 25 minutes
Total: 45 minutes
Release: Naturally
Per Serving: Calories: 98, Protein: 0.7g, Total Fat: 9.9g, Total Carbs: 3.2g, Cholesterol: 0mg, Sodium: 5mg, Potassium: 74mg
Servings: 4

Ingredients:

- 4 chicken breasts, boneless, skinless
- 1 teaspoon minced garlic
- 2 teaspoons olive oil
- ½ teaspoon ground ginger
- ½ teaspoon cinnamon
- ½ teaspoon black pepper
- 1 teaspoon cumin
- 1 green onion, chopped, for garnish

Directions:

- Mix all ingredients in mixing bowl; place in refrigerator overnight to marinate.

- Add ingredients to Instant Pot®. Secure lid, set at 'poultry' and cook for 25 minutes.
- Use natural release. Garnish with green onion and serve.

54. Chicken & Fruit Combo (Low-Carb)

Prep Time: 10 minutes
Setting: Poultry, 25 minutes
Total: 40 minutes
Release: Naturally
Per Serving: Calories: 276, Protein: 28.1g, Total Fat: 7.2g, Total Carbs: 25.5g, Cholesterol: 75mg, Sodium: 112mg, Potassium: 1077mg
Servings: 4

Ingredients:

- ½ cup orange juice, unsweetened
- ½ cup apple pulp
- ½ cup papaya pulp
- ½ cup raspberry juice
- 1 pound chicken breast, skinless, boneless, cut into bite-size pieces
- ½ cup pomegranate juice
- 1 teaspoon pepper
- ½ cup tomato puree

Directions:

- Combine all ingredients in mixing bowl and refrigerate overnight.
- Place in Instant Pot®. Secure lid, set at 'poultry' and cook for 25 minutes.
- Release pressure naturally.
- Serve over bed of rice.

55. Ham & Cabbage (Low-Carb)

Prep Time: 12 minutes
Setting: Meat, 20 minutes
Total: 40 minutes
Release: Quick
Per Serving: Calories: 1,159, Protein: 81.4g, Total Fat: 63.2g, Total Carbs: 65.7g, Cholesterol: 320mg, Sodium: 6165mg, Potassium: 2467mg
Servings: 4

Ingredients:

- 1 pound cooked ham, cut into small pieces
- 1 large carrot, sliced into coins
- 1 teaspoon cumin powder
- 1 teaspoon chili powder
- 1 large potato, chopped
- 1 onion, minced
- Shredded cabbage
- 2 tablespoons melted butter

Directions:

- Combine all ingredients and pour into Instant Pot®. Secure lid, set at 'meat' and cook for 20 minutes.
- Allow pressure to release naturally.

56. Ginger Duck (Low-Carb)

Prep Time: 10 minutes
Setting: Poultry, 40 minutes
Total: 60 minutes
Release: Naturally
Per Serving: Calories: 564, Protein: 54.9g, Total Fat: 25.1g, Total Carbs: 23.8g, Cholesterol: 197mg, Sodium: 249mg, Potassium: 1425mg
Servings: 8

Ingredients:

- 1 duck, properly processed
- 2 carrots, diced
- 1 cucumber, cut into small pieces
- 2 cups water
- 2 tablespoons cooking wine
- 1 inch ginger, chopped
- Salt and pepper to taste

Directions:

- Add duck to Instant Pot® and pour all the other ingredients over it.
- Secure lid, set at 'poultry' and cook for 40 minutes.
- Release pressure naturally.

57. Teriyaki Meatballs (Family Friendly)

Prep Time: 15 minutes
Setting: Meat, 50 minutes
Total: 80 minutes
Release: Quick
Per Serving: Calories: 1,359, Protein: 165.0g, Total Fat: 60.1g, Total Carbs: 32.1g, Cholesterol: 758mg, Sodium: 7779mg, Potassium: 2402mg
Servings: 4

Ingredients:

- 1 teaspoon butter
- 4 ounces finely sliced white onion
- 1 teaspoon minced ginger
- 1 teaspoon minced garlic
- 1 pound ground beef
- 2 eggs
- 1 cup shredded mozzarella cheese
- 1½ teaspoons sea salt
- 4 teaspoons herb seasoning
- 1 teaspoon olive oil

- 4 ounces Teriyaki sauce

Directions:

- Saute the butter, onion, ginger, and garlic in Instant Pot® for 3 minutes.
- Allow to completely cool.
- Place ground beef in a separate bowl; add cooled onion, ginger and garlic, along with eggs, cheese, salt and seasoning.
- Mix well; make 16 small meatballs.
- Place oil in frying pan and brown meatballs on all sides.
- Place in Instant Pot® add in Teriyaki sauce.
- Secure lid, set at 'meat' setting and cook for 50 minutes.

58. Thai Chicken & Cashews (Family Friendly)

Prep Time: 15 minutes
Setting: Poultry, 30 minutes
Total: 45 minutes
Release: Quick
Per Serving: Calories: 1,834, Protein: 21.9g, Total Fat: 174.8g, Total Carbs: 60.3g, Cholesterol: 122mg, Sodium: 404mg, Potassium: 1335mg
Servings: 6

Ingredients:

- 3 chicken breasts, boneless, skinless, cut into small pieces
- 1 cup coconut milk
- 1 cup cauliflower florets
- 1 package frozen mixed veggies
- 4 ounces Thai curry paste
- 4 tablespoons butter
- ½ cup chopped cashews

Directions:

- Place all ingredients into Instant Pot®; secure lid, set at 'poultry' and cook for 30 minutes.
- Use quick release.

59. Chicken & Zucchini (Family Friendly)

Prep Time: 12 minutes
Setting: Poultry, 40 minutes
Total: 65 minutes
Release: Quick
Per Serving: Calories: 770, Protein: 17.0g, Total Fat: 64.4g, Total Carbs: 50.4g, Cholesterol: 0mg, Sodium: 128mg, Potassium: 2926mg
Servings: 8

Ingredients:

- 1 teaspoon coconut oil
- ½ cup diced white onion
- 1 teaspoon minced garlic
- 4 chicken breasts, boneless, skinless, chopped into chunks
- 4 zucchini, finely chopped
- 1 teaspoon garam masala
- ¼ teaspoon cayenne pepper
- ¼ cup chopped, fresh cilantro
- ½ teaspoon cumin
- 1 tablespoon curry powder
- 1 cup coconut milk

Directions:

- Add coconut oil to Instant Pot® along with onion and garlic; sauté for 3 minutes.
- Add remaining ingredients; secure lid, set at 'poultry' and cook for 40 minutes.
- Use quick release and enjoy!

Conclusion

I hope you and your loved ones enjoy preparing this vast collection of Instant Pot® recipes. Your taste buds will come alive while eating healthy meals the whole family enjoys. In this collection, there is something to suit everyone's taste: from the vegetarian to the hearty meat lover to those that love seafood—I am confident everyone will find special recipes in this cookbook to suit their tastes and needs. Nutritional information is included to help those who are trying to watch what they consume (such as cutting back on carbs, for example). You will find plenty of low-carb recipes in this collection which the whole family will love! When you prepare these meals for your loved ones, rest assured in the knowledge you are providing them with deliciously healthy home-cooked meals!

Again, thank you for buying my Instant Pot® cookbook; it is very much appreciated.

If you really enjoyed reading it and using the recipes, please leave a review on Amazon. I would love to read your review of my book!

Thank you and good luck!

Renil M. George

Other Books by Metroconnections Inc. Publishing House:

Focus: The Practical Guide to Improving Your Mental Concentration, Killing Procrastination and Increasing Productivity
(4 Times Best Seller)

Available on Amazon!

Click here to access the book now!!

For hard copy readers, Go to Amazon.com and search for Focus: The Practical Guide to Improving Your Mental Concentration, Killing Procrastination, and Increasing Productivity

To watch the book trailer, click here!!!

https://www.youtube.com/watch?v=WOLs7lx4fQo

Ketogenic Diet Recipes: 50 Delicious, Healthy Low-Carb Ketogenic Recipes, Snacks and Desserts for Weight Loss (Amazing Dinner Recipes and Tips on How to Avoid Diet Mistakes, Book 1)

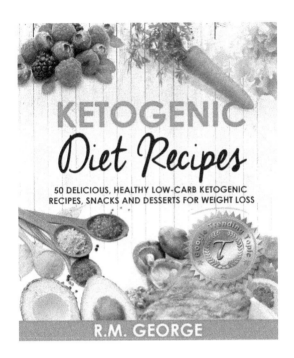

Available on Amazon!

Click here to access the book now!!

For hard copy readers, Go to Amazon.com and search for Ketogenic Diet Recipes: 50 Delicious, Healthy Low-Carb Ketogenic Recipes, Snacks and Desserts for Weight Loss

To watch the book trailer, click here!!!

https://www.youtube.com/watch?v=wupE2oGON6E

CPSIA information can be obtained
at www.ICGtesting.com
Printed in the USA
BVHW012125100219
539925BV00003B/88/P